WORSHIP AND THE CHILD

Worship and the Child

Essays by the Joint Liturgical Group

EDITED BY RONALD C. D. JASPER

LONDON SPCK

First published 1975
by SPCK
Holy Trinity Church
Marylebone Road
London NW1 4DU

Printed in Great Britain by
William Clowes & Sons Limited
London, Colchester and Beccles

SBN 281 02857 5

CONTENTS

ACKNOWLEDGEMENTS

Thanks are due to the following for permission to quote from copyright sources:

General Assembly of the Church of Scotland: extracts from the General Assembly Reports, 1973 and 1974.

Grove Books: *Patterns of Sunday Worship*, by C. O. Buchanan.

H. A. Hamilton: *The Family Church in Principle and Practice*.

THE JOINT LITURGICAL GROUP

MEMBERS

1 **Church of England**
The Reverend D. C. Gray,
The Archdeacon of Westminster
(The Venerable Dr R. C. D. Jasper), *Secretary*

2 **The Church of Scotland**
The Reverend Dr R. S. Louden
Mr F. N. Davidson Kelly

3 **The Baptist Union of Great Britain and Ireland**
The Reverend N. Clark
The Reverend S. F. Winward (until March 1974)
The Reverend M. Williams (after March 1974)

4 **The United Reformed Church**
The Reverend R. A. Davies
The Reverend J. M. Todd

5 **The Episcopal Church in Scotland**
The Reverend Canon A. O. Barkway

6 **The Methodist Church**
The Reverend A. R. George
The Reverend G. S. Wakefield

7 **The Roman Catholic Church**
The Right Reverend Monsignor G. A. Tomlinson
The Reverend H. Winstone

8 **The Churches of Christ**
The Reverend Dr W. G. Baker

STATEMENT OF 11 OCTOBER 1963

Informal discussions on liturgical matters between interested people from various Churches in Great Britain have indicated that the time is now ripe for the creation of a Joint Liturgical Group which can develop given projects and questions of public worship. The Archbishop of Canterbury was asked to help bring such a Group into being by issuing invitations to the Churches concerned to appoint members. His Grace kindly agreed to do so and himself appointed the representatives of the Church of England, while those of other Churches have been appointed by their respective bodies.

At its first meeting on 10–11 October 1963 the Group elected the Dean of Bristol as its Chairman and Dr Jasper as its Secretary.

It is clearly to be understood that any work produced by this Group will have no authority greater than that which its own members give to it by their own weight; but it will be for particular Churches, through their customary modes of decision, to make use of the results if they are willing to do so.

The initial projects which the Group has decided to discuss are these:

1. The planning of a Calendar, Forms of Daily Service, and a Lectionary which the Churches might be glad to have in common.
2. The planning of joint forms of service which might be used with the approval of the several Churches on occasions for united worship, such as the Week of Prayer for Unity and Holy Week.
3. The consideration of the structure of the service of Holy Communion.

Neville Clark

Children, when taken seriously, pose liturgical questions. In our day these questions have become acute, and the Church ignores them at its peril. The liturgy is traditionally an adult preserve. Liturgical reconstruction has tended to proceed without much conscious reference to the child. He emerges as an unconnected pendant, awkward, ill-fitting, somehow painfully to be related to the finished product set before him.

Today the child can no longer be treated in so cavalier a fashion. Theological and educational insights have combined to make such a conclusion inevitable. The Churches travail over him in committee, and spawn paraliturgical forms for his enjoyment. Realism dictates the recognition that effective liturgy is not produced in abstraction from real life, by cogent argument from first principles. Rather does it tend to be the subsequent canonization of what the People of God have over the years become accustomed to do. Nevertheless, it may be elementary wisdom to attempt to think through the issues at stake before *ad hoc* solutions become too deeply embedded to be any longer susceptible to criticism.

The time is surely ripe for such exploration to be conducted in ecumenical fashion. No branch of the Christian Church is wholly untouched by the ferment. The Roman Communion in this country, rocking in the wake of Vatican II, seeks to come to terms with the recent *Directory on Children's Masses*. The Church of England hovers uneasily between the Parish Communion and the Family Service, and debates the relationship between Christian Initiation and Communion. The Church of Scotland looks again at the place of the Sunday school and cautiously examines the case for the admission of children to communion. The Methodist Church is driven to ask whether a mature confession of faith must necessarily precede eucharistic reception. That educational arm of the Free Churches, the British Lessons Council, gropes for new patterns to supersede

Experience and Faith. The British Council of Churches Consultative Group on Ministry among Children sets up a working party on *The Child in the Church.*

Whatever may be the flavour of the resultant potpourri, the pervasive nature of the concern is plain. Perspectives, however, remain critically significant. A problem posed within a denominational context will not remain exactly the same when plotted from an ecumenical standpoint. A question asked from an educational perspective may find itself reframed when a liturgical point of reference is invoked. There may then be value in speaking deliberately and explicitly of 'worship and the child', and seeking from that central vantage point to expose for discussion some key issues and provisional judgements.

1. Liturgical forms may rightly be many. Yet to a Christian community set in place, in time, in locality, belongs one liturgy, one worship. There is not one liturgy for men, another for women, another for children. There is the one liturgical drama for the one People of God. The degree and level of participation may vary; but it is the same reality in which all, in one way or another, are to be involved.

The making of such an affirmation does not of itself settle all the practical questions. It does not necessarily imply that children should receive communion or be present at the proclamation of the Word. It does, however, circumscribe the terms of the argument. It delimits the nature of the options. And it poses some fresh questions.

Are children to be introduced to the worship of the People of God by ushering them into some specially created children's or family service? Perhaps the answer will depend on the informing aims and the governing purposes. It would be liturgical purism of the worst kind to insist that every experience of worship should be of the Liturgy of Word and Supper. The life of the Church is not to be canalized in so rigid a fashion.

Yet paraliturgical forms are not the Liturgy. Too often the diversion of children into other forms of worship is based on two disastrous misconceptions. The one is that the Liturgy is for adults only. The other is that the child is merely an adult in the making. Certainly he is an adult in the making. But he is more. He is a member of the family, a unit within the community. And the Liturgy is not only that towards which he moves. It is also that in which, in some measure, he should participate.

So it is that the traffic must be two-way. On the one hand it is the Liturgy that provides the controlling norms for the activity of worship in which the child is to be involved. The pillars of the Liturgy are not to be overturned on the plea that something different and more suitable must be provided for the child. Yet, on the other hand, real questions raised on behalf of the child must be allowed to speak seriously to liturgical practice. They must not too quickly be brushed aside as of no account.

Perhaps the most obvious of them is the question of participation. Almost every service created for children regards it as axiomatic that those present must 'take a part'. Is this assumption justified? If it is, then it must be allowed to menace any other hallowed way of doing the Liturgy. It cannot necessarily be explained away as just a characteristic of children. Either way, what would be disastrous would be the introduction of participation into the Liturgy simply and solely for children. If it is right for children to use responsive prayers it is right for adults. If it is right for the child to 'take a part' it is right for the parent. And only if he does so will the thrust of the Liturgy remain unitive rather than divisive.

2. It might seem that nothing has done more to support this understanding of the one Liturgy for all ages than the recent dominance of the concept of the Church as a family. Family Services for a Family Church! What could be truer and less unexceptionable than that?

Certainly the emergence of this understanding has been of profound value, and our contemporary church life is the debtor. Under the impetus of this family concept herculean efforts have been made to bridge the gulf between Sunday school and church and to bring back the child from the circumference of the community to its centre. Insights gained in and revealed by family life have been taken up and applied to the life and worship of the People of God with astonishing fruitfulness. In uncounted ways the result has been for good.

It has, however, to be asked whether at the same time the seeds of potential disaster have not all too lightly been sown. The term family comes to our modern ears laden with a mountain of psychological and sociological baggage. All too rarely has it been subjected to searching and discriminating theological inquiry. It chimed in with the contemporary mood only too easily and well. Given proper provisos there may be much to be welcomed and little to be feared in manifestations of popular religion. The all-important proviso is that they be thoroughly and sensitively baptized into a deeply Christian faith and understanding.

Wherein does the peril lie? It is to be located particularly at two points. More and more the popular conception of the family (at least in the circles that impinge upon the Church) gives a central and determinative place to the children. Whether this is wise, balanced, or even helpful to the child is not the point at issue. The immediate question that has to be faced is whether the acceptance of such an understanding does not critically distort the definitively Christian images of the Church.

That is one peril. The other resides in the heavily emotional coloration which is inherent in the contemporary image of the family. This is bound up with the affective ties which provide it with its natural rooting and coherence. Whether the heavy modern emphasis given to this point ministers to the essential health and stability of the family is again not the point at issue. What has to be asked is whether the heart of the Church is validly unveiled in such categories.

It may be suggested that the signs are not auspicious. A close look at some of the current pressures upon the Church in the name of family worship might well quickly lay bare splurges of sentimental emotionalism clustering round the enthroned child. What is required is not wholesale approval or wholesale condemnation. It is rather a searching return to the New Testament image which is so closely related to that of the family and yet so subtly different—the image of the household of God, the household of the faith.

3. The introduction of Scripture as a corrective to modern enthusiasms points to the third issue that has to be tabled. It is the question of the proper use of the Bible. If it is the view of the Church as Family that has vastly encouraged the presence of children at the celebration of the Supper it is problems associated with Scripture

that have helped to promote their removal from the proclamation of the Word.

We have constantly been reminded that the Bible is not a children's book. In many respects that is a true judgement. It was perhaps inevitable not only that the tendency to withdraw the child from that part of the Liturgy where Scripture was especially dominant should be accentuated but also that embarrassment over the use of Scripture with children should grow.

It must be questioned how far anything like a satisfactory solution could emerge at this point in so far as the context of inquiry remained the 'special service' or the 'departmental meeting'. The use of the Bible can with difficulty be read off from a situation created for children or heavily structured for teaching purposes. Inevitably— and rightly—it was concluded that the starting point must be experience. It was not so clear how Scripture was supposed to operate. It was a source of illustration. It could provide material bearing upon some common theme. It might occasionally provide a religious answer to a human question. Could it do much else?

Perhaps it has to be asked to what extent the Bible is really at home within the educational setting. That it may be used for teaching purposes need not be denied. Yet such a use is always secondary, subservient, dependent upon a primary use that must remain controlling. Scripture is essentially the normative tradition of a community. Certainly it is not a private and esoteric possession. The community bears it for all men. Yet its meaningful rooting is within that community, and in particular at the place where the community at worship, set between remembrance and hope, celebrates the presence and coming of God.

It cannot be assumed that the setting forth of the Word within the Liturgy of the Church always or commonly reflects such an understanding. Alien models of the use of Scripture have long since affected worship itself. Nevertheless, the important task may be to establish the primary use of Scripture, and then to ensure that that use is faithfully reflected in any employment of the Bible with children. Here, once more, what begins as a question posed to the Church by the child may end as a problem upon whose right solution the health of the whole community depends.

The attempt has here been made to raise some fundamental questions, to diagnose some of the perils, to suggest some directions of advance. The denominational statements that follow chart in more detail the situation for today and the debates for tomorrow. The final programmatic essay seeks both to argue a case and to stimulate discussion. Solutions at many points still lie over the horizon. It remains important that they be found.

Donald Gray

THE BACKGROUND

Until twenty years ago it would have been accepted, almost without question, that the Sunday programme of any Church of England parish would contain the properly allocated time for a Sunday school. The vast majority of these Sunday schools would meet in the afternoons, although a few would assemble in the mornings and in the 1950s there would still be a few (but a rapidly declining number) who would meet on both Sunday afternoon and in the morning. Today the truth is that there is no longer any such unified pattern in the instruction of the Church's children, indeed there is a whole host of possibilities.

The most significant change has been that many parishes have come to a realization that children ought not to be isolated from the rest of the worshipping family of the Church.

It is a fact that in the past the Sunday school and its various activities was thought to be a sufficient diet for the children. It was not an unfair criticism, particularly in the north of England, that the Church and the Sunday school lived quite separate lives which only rarely overlapped. Although each session of the Sunday school would have its acts of opening and closing worship, which would perhaps be an amalgam of specially prepared children's prayer and some suitable extracts from the Prayer Book, the children would find it difficult to relate this experience to what they knew of the worship of their parish church.

Significantly in the majority of parishes the Sunday school classes took place somewhere apart from the church building. Yet there was a tradition in some places that on one Sunday in each month (usually the first) the Sunday school would go to the church at the usual Sunday school time for a service. In those places where they were not a monthly occurrence such services were, however, usually held at Christmas, Mothering Sunday, Easter, Whitsuntide, and

Harvest, and on these occasions parents would be invited and a significant number would take part.

In many parishes the one guaranteed time that young people would be found attending the normal morning service in any appreciable numbers would be for the church parade of the parish's uniformed organizations (Scouts, Guides, CLB, CGB, etc.). This Parade Sunday would usually be a monthly occasion.

THE DEVELOPMENT OF THE PARISH COMMUNION

The first signs of any really significant change of policy in the relating of children to the parish's worship came as more and more parishes fell under the influence of the Parish Communion.[1]

This was the Anglican response to the Liturgical Movement. The emphasis was now to be on a Communion service which would involve all sections of the parish. Instead of the parish being divided up into groups meeting for worship either at the 8 o'clock or the 11 o'clock services the congregation was encouraged to gather together for one service which was to be as complete an offering of worship as possible and usually held mid-morning. This one act of worship was to be that service which our Lord himself instituted and the battle cry was, 'The Lord's Service for the Lord's people on the Lord's Day'.

Families were encouraged to come together to this Parish Communion service (it was often called a *Family* Communion or Eucharist) with a consequent decline in the attendance at the afternoon Sunday school. About the same time a sociological factor was added. The family car became common and Sunday afternoons, particularly in the spring and summer, became a favourite time for a 'run-out'. There was now an almost complete collapse of the Sunday afternoon classes in urban areas. Today, the Sunday afternoon Sunday school is perhaps only to be found in the country.

There were those who saw dangers in this sudden decline of the Sunday school and questioned whether or not children would now receive the religious instruction they needed. Although they received regular lessons in their day schools according to the Agreed Syllabus there was still need, many church people felt, for specific 'church'

[1] *The Parish Communion Today*, ed. D. M. Paton (SPCK 1962), reviewed the development of the service over twenty-five years.

instruction. Some parishes moved the instruction from Sunday to another day in the week. 'Sunday school clubs' meeting on a weekday evening or Saturday morning replaced the more traditional pattern. But more commonly parishes which had adopted the Parish Communion now began a number of methods of dealing with the instruction of children in close conjunction with their new form of Sunday worship.

CHILDREN AT THE PARISH COMMUNION

In some places the children assembled with the whole congregation at the beginning of the service but left the church to receive their own instruction when the sermon was reached and remained in their classes until the end of the service. Occasionally the children left church just for the period of the sermon. This method depended on there being suitable rooms conveniently near to the church. But it was a method which usually provoked not unreasonable complaints from the Sunday school teachers that the seven-minute Parish Communion-type sermon gave them no time to develop a theme for the benefit of the children.

The other widely adopted method is one in which the children assemble for their own instruction in their own location and then join the rest of the congregation during the course of the service. The most favoured point of entry is the Offertory. This means that the children can join with the adults for the whole of the eucharistic action having had their own Ministry of the Word in their own classes and at their own level. There is the further advantage in this timing in that the children are then able to be present for the most visually interesting parts of the service. Further, in the majority of places in which the children are present at this point in the service additional participation in the action is possible by the children themselves going to the altar rail at the time of communion to receive a blessing.

This particular point of participation of children in the Communion service has been welcomed by those who have noted a significant fall-away among the recently confirmed; for the simple reason that many young people experience acute embarrassment (at an age when they are sensitive to such situations) at the apparently simple act of walking up and returning through the congregation to make their communion. There would seem to be evidence that those children who over a number of years have become used to going forward to kneel at the communion rail for a blessing do not experience this problem of embarrassment when they come to be confirmed.

The blessing received at the altar rail while others are receiving the Holy Communion is intended to make clear to the children their acceptance in the total life of the Christian family. However, there are many clergy and laypeople (particularly those who have a responsibility for the training of children) who find that this action, seemingly simple and direct, tends to highlight the Church of England's confusion about membership and communion.

If indeed the children are members of the church by their baptism and are fit to approach so near to the altar, why are they then denied the token of their membership? If it is being argued that children could not *understand* what they are doing in receiving the eucharistic gifts, then we as adults are making the most arrogant claims about our own understanding of what can only be described as one of the most profound of all mysteries. Surely we have begun to learn that it is folly to try and simplify the Eucharist into the inadequacies of human description.

Even so it seems to be that the thought-forms of the child are more often able to pierce the fog of theological debate which too often surrounds our talk about the Holy Communion. For them there is no difficulty in 'discerning the Lord'.

The sacramental principle is not one which is as foreign to the child's mind as it is to many sophisticated adults. For the child, play and make-believe, reality and facts, overlap and interplay indiscriminately. This is *not* in any sense to suggest that what we are doing in the Eucharist is make-believe but the very lack of precision and exactness in our descriptions of what we are doing, what we receive, do not invalidate the action for the child (or the child-like?).

These are some of the factors which colour the recommendations of the Ely Report on Christian Initiation which is discussed under 'Future Developments' (pp. 20–1 below).

THE NON-EUCHARISTIC FAMILY SERVICE

In the last few years there have been those who have criticized the Parish Communion movement because it has encouraged a form of service which they would say is too exclusive. Unconfirmed adults are said to be discouraged from attendance because of their inability to receive communion. The casual unconfirmed visitor and his family do not return after one non-communicating experience. For this reason in a number of parishes, particularly in new housing areas, a form of family service has been developed which is not a Communion service. This type of service is said better to serve the pastoral and evangelistic needs of this kind of developing area. In fact, the Church of England Liturgical Commission has been under constant pressure to produce such a non-eucharistic service. The Commission has resisted this and suggested that local circumstances can best provide the stimulus for this kind of local liturgical expression.

These family services are highly informal with a good deal of congregational participation. The children are present throughout and sometimes the service has the ingredients of a 'Children's Church' in which the children play the roles and functions of church officers and lead parts of the service. In some parishes the form of service does include parts of the Communion service and is intended to be a half-way house to the Parish Communion.

The non-eucharistic family service is a weekly feature of some parish programmes, but in some it alternates with some other morning service, in others it is a monthly feature.

THE CHILDREN'S EUCHARIST

Recently in a number of parishes there has been a return to a practice of the early twentieth-century Tractarians of holding a Children's Mass. This is a Eucharist which is interspersed with spoken explanations which help the children to understand the action. A teacher or other adult is positioned in the middle of the children and provides the commentary and helps to lead the responses and the congregational parts of the service. The fullest participation by the young people will be expected and they provide the choir, servers, and even readers. This is essentially a children's service, as its name suggests, and has all the inherent dangers of becoming an end in itself and being a service which the children can grow out of.

AGREEMENT ACROSS THE 'CHURCHMANSHIP' BARRIERS

The one underlying aim of all these methods is a desire to teach children the value of worship in the fellowship of the Church. The main division in the Church of England is whether this is best done through an experience of the Eucharist or in some kind of specially devised family service. The advocates of both methods can now be found in both the main 'churchmanship' traditions of the Church of England. It being no longer true that a eucharistic-centred Sunday pattern is the sole preserve of the High Church tradition, as witness C. O. Buchanan's recently published *Patterns of Sunday Worship*[2] in which he says unhesitatingly of the Parish Communion, that 'we can be sure that no other pattern of the main service of Sunday will serve as well in the future'. An Evangelical, he is convinced of the necessity of providing for the children.

It is usual to set up the Parish Communion in such a way that children can be present at it. Part of its charm and theological integrity is its bringing together of the family for an activity which is not avowedly or implicitly childish, but is not exclusive of children in the way the traditional Morning Prayer has tended to be. Indeed the combination of singing, word, spectacle and action is well adapted psychologically to involving children's attention and interest throughout.

He also believes that they can make a very real contribution to the atmosphere of the service:

Children can do us a good turn by helping us unfreeze the liturgy —one of the astonishing things about evangelicals is that they like informal prayer meetings, they like informal fellowship, they like warmth—but they loathe all these at the communion! What more natural and proper place, in the economy of God, for them?

FUTURE DEVELOPMENTS

The pattern for the future is not easy to forecast. The Church of England is at present engaged in a prolonged discussion about Christian Initiation.[3] This involves not only the rights and wrongs

[2] Grove Booklets on Ministry and Worship No. 9, 1972.
[3] See *Christian Initiation. Birth and Growth in Christian Society* (CIO 1971).

of Infant Baptism but also questions about the right age at which children ought to start to receive communion.

The outcome of this debate could be the earlier admission of children to Holy Communion, by separating the traditional Anglican connection between Confirmation and Communion. Either Confirmation could be united with water baptism and be administered in infancy or children could start to receive communion at an earlier age than the traditional Anglican 12–15-year-old range and be confirmed later. This earlier reception would be preceded by instruction, but such preparation would not be couched in the 'life-vows' terms that much Confirmation teaching has contained in the past.

Any such changes in communion discipline would require some subsequent changes in the arrangement of Sunday worship in many Church of England parishes.

3 A CHURCH OF SCOTLAND POINT OF VIEW

R. Stuart Louden

The place of children and young people in the life of the Church of Scotland and at public worship was traditionally based on the family as the essential social unit. Before the modern Communion Rolls arose in Scottish parishes there were lists of 'Heads of houses'. The role of those paterfamilias in the Scottish church-home included responsibility for the religious training of children and servants; for example, the farmer in the 'farm-toun' had not only his own children but also his farm-servants and their families within his paternalistic spiritual care. In a Scotland where the parish kirks were locked up between Lord's Days, the spiritual centre of week-day life was held to rest in family worship, and at the family altar were found such elements as there were of what would now be termed the religious instruction of youth.

In regard to participation in the Lord's Supper, it was also the heads of houses who had to be satisfied that would-be communicants were knowledgeable in the Belief (the Apostles' Creed), the Lord's Prayer, and the Sum of the Law (the Ten Commandments), and thus able 'to discern the Lord's body'. This may have resulted in an unfortunate reluctance to receive Holy Communion, but it also contributed elevated spiritual emphasis to the solemn step taken by an individual in presuming to partake of the bread and the wine. Scottish Church practice in general has tended to be related more to a paternalist Christian society than to the modern secular and pluralist society or to rampant individualism.

When today we endeavour to evaluate the Sunday school, the Bible class, and religious education, it is relevant to note that all these arose within patterns of society in the epoch following the Industrial Revolution. This type of modern industrial society is more and more characteristic of the whole people, and is common to both rural and town life. It has meant that the family as the basic unit of human society has become less and less important, and has even tended to be obliterated. The Sunday school movement, even in its undoubted achievements and contribution, has nevertheless been a token of the weakening of Christian family life.

By 1900 the Church of Scotland in its divided parts was practising a well-organized system of Bible-teaching in the Sunday school and the so-called 'Bible Class'. Speaking generally the children of school age were instructed in the Sunday schools, while the Bible classes, junior and senior, provided teaching which was mainly scriptural rather than doctrinal or churchly, for young people over school age up to quite senior levels among young adults. Such teaching was always given in the context of a simple act of worship. There was always a proportion of children and young persons who had no personal experience of public worship except at the Sunday school or the Bible class. Somewhere within this at first loosely organized system of Bible-teaching, religious training, and simple worship, there was a 'Minister's Class in Preparation for First Communion' before any adherent of the congregation was admitted to participation in the sacrament of the Lord's Supper. Until comparatively recently this seldom happened before the age of eighteen.

Interestingly enough it was from pedagogic circles and under the pressure of modern teaching methods, that the Sunday schools developed into their current efficient and well-organized departments geared to the age and abilities of the children: beginners (under school age); primary (ages 5 to 8); juniors (ages 9 to 11/12); seniors (ages 12 to 14/15). This greater relevance and competence in Sunday school teaching, however, increased the tendency for the Sunday school to become an autonomous centre of worship and Christian training. In terms of the Sunday programme, parents and children began to face an unfortunate conflict and choice between church-going and Sunday school attendance. The very success of the modern Sunday school movement has created many of the problems now facing the Church in regard to participation in public worship by the young.

The Bible class movement in size and effectiveness is now a mere shadow of its earlier influence and strength. An exception is the Boys' Brigade Bible class, an essential element in that particular uniformed youth organization, and it remains a valuable element in the Scottish Church's religious training, although it is difficult to establish what support, if any, it gives to attendance at public worship.

In the years since the Second World War, the earlier maturing of school children and a variety of other causes have resulted in a large-scale drop in the numbers attending our Sunday schools. This same period has also been marked by growing uneasiness in the Church over exclusively Bible-teaching, sometimes with a crudely scriptural bias, and the older accepted lesson schemes have been widely criticized. This was perhaps an inevitable consequence of a teaching situation where methodology had been allowed to become more influential than doctrinal content. Developing theological positions and changes in biblical interpretation have also played their part in the unease.

The Church of Scotland has for long co-operated with the Scottish Sunday School Union for Christian Education in preparing Sunday school lesson material. The form of this co-operation was revised and improved in 1926, but since the Second World War there has been a growing conviction that more doctrinal and church-centred teaching material was required. With the help of the Baird Research Fellow, the Church of Scotland has produced more churchly material for use in the Sunday school. Clearly this of itself will not stem the decline in numbers, or resolve deeper questions about the place of the Sunday school and the Bible class in relation to attendance at public worship and communicant church member-ship.

The General Assembly's Committee on Religious Instruction of Youth has been renamed the Committee on Parish Education and has received a redefined and more relevant remit from the General Assembly. The Division on Children within this Committee on Parish Education is sponsoring a Working Party to: '(i) determine the place of Sunday Schools and Bible Classes in the life of congrega-tions, and (ii) find ways in which the local Church family can implement its responsibilities to its children' (General Assembly Reports, 1974).

Turning now from the religious impact centred in the home or in the Sunday school and Bible class, specific attention must also be given to developments within the Church's public worship itself over the past century. There have been a variety of efforts to give the child and young person a more congenial and appropriate place in the worshipping congregation. The inclusion of children's hymns in the *Church Hymnary* (1898, 1927, and 1973) is token that the young were expected to be involved in regular public worship.

'Children's Services' were a feature for many decades, often closely linked to the activities and teaching of the Sunday school. Such special services were intended to be a training ground for adult church worship, and they were at one time very effective and valuable occasions of worship in themselves. The children's service was usually a form of worship reflecting the sequence and content of the ordinary divine service. The form was often made more interesting than the adults' canonical occasion by the inclusion of responsive material and 'audience participation' in shorter and more varied devotional forms. Responsive readings, litanies, repetition of the Creed and the like were included in those children's services with the purpose of making public worship more lively, interesting, and varied for the young. It should be noted that in the Book of Common Order, 1940, three services for children are included, but it is probable that these are now never used.

This particular 'Children's Service' tradition has also ended for changing sociological reasons: an alternative or additional hour of worship, peculiarly for the children, is not attainable in the busy, and 'holiday', Lord's Day. The pedagogic element, directed towards later full participation in the Church's public worship, is a very considerable loss. Moreover, the loss by the Church of its claims on a great part of Sunday has meant the Sunday school being more and more integrated into the one main hour of public worship, in Scotland the canonical hour of 11 o'clock. Sunday schools now mostly take place during morning church, either meeting at the same hour, or having the children and their teachers go out from the church service after one of the Scripture lessons or at another convenient point. On the credit side, this particular change from a wholly separate hour for Sunday school has helped to reverse the damaging tendency of too wide separation between church worship and an over-autonomous Sunday school. But, alas, this has been happening at the very time when the Sunday school movement itself is declining.

Note has also to be taken of the 'Children's Address' which in some congregations of the Church of Scotland has been a notable feature in public worship for many decades, and was probably at the height of its vogue between the Wars. In practice, the popular preacher tended to vie with himself in making the children's address as absorbing and remarkable as the sermon proper. Adults in the congregation tended to look to that part of the service for light relief through gentle humour or acute gimmick. There is little evidence to suggest that the children's address brought to public worship any children who would not have been brought there in any case, while extravagant adult appreciation of this element in the church service only suggested other weaknesses and lacks in the general tradition of Scottish preaching.

Those liturgically concerned and sensitive object to the children's address because of its intrusion into the sequence of public worship, the place where it is given being an entirely arbitrary local choice. A few moments of 'light relief' after the prayers of approach or after one of the Scripture lessons can make no contribution to the meaningful order and sequence of a church service, while its mood may be damaging to reverence in worship and to the majesty of preaching as the proclamation of the Word of God. This problem of intrusion in regard to the children's address has become even more acute since the ordered eucharistic pattern of public worship has been so widely adopted on an ecumenical basis.

Churches can learn from the failure in success of the children's address that the teaching element, greater simplicity and practical illustration, should have a larger place in the central kerygma of the Church of God. What, at its best, both children and adults derived of help from the children's address should be built into the structure, pattern, and content of eucharistic worship. It becomes ever clearer that public worship in the sense of the one main canonical Sunday hour in each denomination, essentially a eucharistic act of worship, is today the one centre at which not only church members as a whole, but children and young people in particular, are ever likely to be gathered together.

The adoption of a eucharistic structure for the main Sunday service in the Church of Scotland presents little difficulty since it is virtually a return to the basic 'Reformed' pattern of public worship. The basic sequence of an early Presbyterian act of worship, based on the medieval Mass, revolved round two points related to the Preaching of the Word: (i) confession of sin before sermon; (ii) prayer and intercession after sermon (cf. John Knox's Liturgy Book of Common Order 1565). In many quarters the 'Long Prayer' after sermon continued this general pattern of the 'dry mass'! An 'Alternative Order' for morning service, in the Book of Common Order, 1940, indicates a ready acceptance of the eucharistic structure, and its use is becoming steadily more widespread. The publication of the *Church Hymnary: Third Edition*, in 1973, probably the first book of praise anywhere to offer its material in a liturgical arrangement, is also extending this eucharistic norm for Church of Scotland practice. The three main sections of this hymnary are entitled: (I) Approach to God; (II) The Word of God:His Mighty Acts; (III) Response to the Word of God.

The fresh and relevant emphasis in the Church of Scotland and in all churches on the eucharistic assembly or the congregation gathered for public worship raises new issues in regard to Christian education and religious instruction. This purpose will have to be more and more promoted through the main people's service on the Lord's Day. The baptized are part of the church family along with the confirmed, and how are all to be instructed as well as spiritually nourished together? The smaller Sunday schools and now almost defunct Bible classes can only exercise an ancillary and marginal influence, while the minister's class in preparation for first communion will perhaps become a less decisive moment, though a continuing important element of training in a young believer's Christian life and commitment. It is the liturgical revision of the Church of Scotland service of Confirmation and Admission to the Lord's Supper which now plays the largest part in ensuring that the approach to first communion is a decisive spiritual moment (Committee on Public Worship and Aids to Devotion, 1969). The traditional distinction between the liturgy of the catechumens and the liturgy of the faithful has virtually been lost in modern church life. As the emphasis on the Church as the eucharistic community develops, it will become ever more difficult to withhold the bread and wine from the baptized who are present at the divine service, whether or not confirmed and admitted to the Lord's Table.

There is an old Scottish tradition of children being present in

church at the former infrequent and most solemn services of Holy
Communion. They were in church but kept apart; sombrely
ignored; present only in an 'observer' role; and, if there was a
gallery in the church, they were conveniently seated in the pews of the
loft, where the elements of bread and wine were not being served.
My own childhood memory is of being an intruder and of having to
be 'very good'! For a generation now some more 'advanced' parents
have brought their children to sit with them in their pew at a Communion service in church, the children just being passed over in the
distribution of the bread and the wine. It is to be noted that perhaps
the majority of those coming to their first communion in the Church
of Scotland have not been present in church at a Eucharist until that
first occasion of their own communicating.

A Special Committee of the General Assembly Anent Church
Membership has posed various searching questions in relation to
this situation:

> Does the theology of Confirmation imply that, in some sense,
> Baptism is incomplete until it is confirmed? Is Confirmation neces-
> sary before Admission to the Lord's Supper? Must Admission
> depend on a single, formal confession of faith and commitment
> for life, or can it depend on an appropriate confession of faith
> before each Communion, as, in the past, catechising took place
> before each Communion? If the latter, can any lower age limit
> be fixed, below which it would be reasonable to assume that a
> child would be incapable of real personal faith in Jesus Christ?
> If a child is capable of real faith, is it right to exclude him from
> the benefits of Communion as a means of grace, and if so, what are
> the actual grounds of such exclusion? For example, must he be
> old enough to ratify baptismal vows made on his behalf, to
> dedicate himself to the service of God, or to testify to a personal
> experience of Jesus Christ and His saving power? Or can these
> things be postponed until a Confirmation after admission to
> Communion? (General Assembly Reports, 1973).

The Church of Scotland is not alone in discerning that today
'there is at least a prima facie case for a careful look at the possibility
of admitting children to Communion'. This brings a wholly new
dimension into our discussion of the place of children in public

worship. In traditional Scottish parlance, the Lord's Supper is a 'converting ordinance' but whatever decisions are made on this issue of admitting children to Holy Communion, the place of religious instruction in the life of congregations has yet to be imaginatively reconstructed, with due recognition of modern sociological patterns and to ensure the presence of all ages in the church family at the main act of public worship and eucharistic assembly.

The Church as a whole has rediscovered, in the eucharistic structure of basic Christian worship, a fresh sense of relevance and meaning in its essential nature as the eucharistic assembly. Children and young people, as well as adults, must share in these new insights, and their place in public worship and how they are instructed in church membership must be vitally related to this liturgical situation. The 'intrusion' into the meaningful sequence of public worship of elements peculiarly and exclusively for the young is no longer helpful or relevant. In hymnody, for example, adults should find themselves singing so-called children's hymns while the young should be learning and joining in the great hymns of the Church. Perhaps the Church will find ways of recreating the Christian family, in its spiritual and liturgical as well as its sociological significance; and then of integrating all ages as a family into the meaningful corporate worship of the Church, the family of God. This inclusive corporate public worship, it is agreed, is essentially eucharistic worship.

4 A ROMAN CATHOLIC POINT OF VIEW

Harold Winstone

The whole question of children's liturgies is relatively new in this country so far as the Roman Catholic Church is concerned, and whatever structures do exist are in a state of flux. It was only after the Second Vatican Council that any serious thought was given to the problem, and then mainly in Catholic schools, not so much in parishes. Before the Council 'active participation' meant no more that taking part in a 'Dialogue Mass', which entailed making the various responses and reciting or singing such things as the Gloria and Credo in Latin.

Since the translation of the Latin Mass into English, however, a great deal has been done, slowly at first, but gradually increasing in momentum. It would now be hard to find a Catholic school where an imaginative and well-prepared 'Classroom Mass' was not part of the regular programme for the term. In such Masses the children play a very substantial part. They help to prepare the room and the altar-table for the Mass. The theme of the Mass is probably taken from their current work in religious education. They prepare simplified readings and perhaps dramatize them, write their own intercessions, choose the hymns, and learn to accompany them on musical instruments. At the Offertory they may bring to the altar and present to God some of the best examples of their school work or the end-product of some project they have all worked on together. In fact, everything is being done to ensure maximum involvement and participation on the part of the children.

The reason for this development is to be sought in the training colleges and catechetical centres. Until recently it has had little active support from some of the hierarchy and many priests are still reluctant to change rubrics or adapt liturgical prayers to the mentality of children. Educationists, however, have begun to apply to liturgy the various psychological and educational principles emerging from their study of their particular disciplines.

Psychologically, they stress the need for the child to develop a positive self-concept—the need to be accepted as he is and be allowed to express himself as a not unimportant member of the community. This postulates a willingness on the part of the adult community of believers to receive him at his faith level. Moreover, the child must identify with a particular group and be assured of belonging; worship with a community is an excellent means of achieving this.

A child needs to believe and to trust. The young child looks for guidance, and depends on the adult to guide him. A mentally retarded child possesses these qualities to a high degree. Church members, therefore, must be prepared to extend themselves to fulfil as best they can these spiritual needs, bearing in mind this characteristic of dependency.

If children are to be able to receive the word and to celebrate the Eucharist they need to become as involved as possible both in body —through words, song, dance, gesture, and music—and in mind— through silence, reflection, listening, and sharing. This again demands on the part of the celebrant and the adult community an attitude of openness, to allow the children to express themselves within the sacred environment.

From the educational point of view it is regarded as axiomatic that the message of the word be translated into terms that are realistic and close to the life-experience of the child. Abstract concepts are little understood by the very young. The mentally retarded have no chance at all of understanding them. For them an intuitive approach is absolutely essential. The message must be experienced and related to their social age. Gestures and movement are an essential concomitant of prayer and song. One can reach their minds only through the emotions and sensibility of the heart.

The child's relatively short attention-span is another factor that must be borne in mind. It forces the educator to present the message in a form that is highly motivating, and to present the Liturgy as the celebration of a life-theme within the child's experience. The personality of the teacher or celebrant must be warm and accepting, and he must be able to communicate with the particular age-group with whom he is celebrating.

The result of this application of educational psychology to the sphere of worship has meant that most children nowadays find the celebration of a school Mass an enjoyable experience. This very fact puts a heavy burden of responsibility on the parish clergy, for if their liturgy is unimaginative and wholly geared to adults, then children are going to find the Sunday Mass by contrast intolerably boring and they will probably resist the attempts of their parents to make them attend church.

This is presenting a serious problem to the Roman Catholic Church in this country and one which cannot for long be ignored. Some parishes have special Children's Masses on Sundays. Only a few have a separate Service of the Word specially adapted to a particular age-group. Even where this is the case the contrast between what goes on in school and what goes on in church is beginning to be very marked.

The problem is clearly exacerbated by the one-sidedness of the approach to its solution. Most of the thinking and experimentation is going on in educational circles and not in the Church as a whole. This is creating an imbalance which may prove damaging in the long run. However much the educationist may say that he is preparing the children gradually to take part in adult parish worship, the fact is that the older the children get the more they begin to complain of the inadequacy, if not irrelevance, of much that goes on in most churches. They complain that it is not even really an adult liturgy, for they are treated as children used to be treated. The scene is dominated by the priest and they have nothing to do except to pay attention to what is being said and done and to repeat all together pre-programmed responses and prayers.

In other words, the time is overdue for a rethinking of the problem at every level. Christian liturgy must be basically unitive. It must not be allowed to become in any sense divisive. In Christ, St Paul says, there is neither Greek nor Jew, male nor female, slave nor freeman. He could also have said 'neither adult nor child'. One may quite readily grant that our supposedly adult liturgies are not apt for the participation of children, but one should also question very seriously whether this is so precisely because they are adult liturgies. May not the reason be that they have become so impoverished that they no longer contain the full richness of human and Christian experience? Children are accepted into ordinary family life and have an appropriate place there, which they tend not to have in the united family worship of the Church.

One further recent development needs comment. Since the Vatican Council many devotional, non-eucharistic services, which were once very popular and formed part of the Catholic's experience of worship, have fallen out of common use. Catholics now tend to identify all liturgy with the celebration of the Eucharist. The ancient Church, however, had a wealth of catechumenal prayers and blessings and community practices of a religious character which were considered an essential part of the preparation for Christian celebration in the Eucharist. Perhaps more should be done on these lines today. Certainly one cannot conceive of a healthy liturgical state *vis-à-vis* children without something being done in the home. The importance of family worship cannot be overestimated. And yet at the present time very little is being done in a sustained way.

Into this situation has recently arrived from the Roman Congregation for Divine Worship an official *Directory on Children's Masses* (dated 1 November 1973). Directory, in Roman Catholic parlance, means a code of directions on how to set about doing something. It is heralded as a school liturgist's charter in that it at last gives official sanction to many practices which were hitherto disallowed, or at least frowned upon, by authority. But it is more than this. It reviews the whole field of children in relation to their worship and is the result of four years' intensive study of the problem by an international team of experts. It is, moreover, to be regarded as a supplement to the General Instruction which prefaces the new Roman Missal giving detailed pastoral instructions on the celebration of Mass.

It would be totally misleading to suggest that this Directory represents the present state of children's worship in the Roman Catholic Church in this country. It will possibly take many years for these ideas to sink in at parish level, and many more years before a proper integration of liturgical practice in the home, the school, and the church is achieved. But it is nevertheless an important document and one which will have a considerable influence on the future celebration of liturgy.

It begins by enumerating those 'human values' which underly all forms of community worship. Such human values are the exchange of greetings, the capacity to listen, to forgive, and to ask for forgiveness, the expression of gratitude, the use of signs and symbols to express abstract concepts, and the human need to celebrate in a festive, convivial way. By learning these human values and experiencing them in the home and in his relationship with other people, the child is also learning the fundamental elements of liturgy in the assembly which brings the faithful together to celebrate the paschal mystery. The aim, therefore, of eucharistic catechesis should be to cultivate in the child these human values. His degree of participation in worship will then keep pace with his psychological and social development. Before he is expected to take part in the full worship of the community, he can share with other children in simple acts of worship which express one or other of the human values we have described. Simple services of this kind can be scripturally based and made joyful and involving. One must, however, resist the temptation to make them too didactic.

Catechesis must also aim at conveying to the child through the medium of the principal rites and prayers an understanding of the Eucharist as a sharing in the life of the whole Church. Similarly preparation for the first communion: the aim will be not merely to instruct the child in the truths of the faith concerning the Eucharist, but also to explain how he is going henceforth to have a fully active part in the celebration of the Eucharist by sharing in the Lord's table with the community of fellow-believers.

Since the reforms of Pope Pius X, 'the age of discretion' has been universally regarded as the approprite time for children to make their first Holy Communion. This is interpreted as meaning about the age of seven, but it is for the parent to decide when their child is ready. Until recently each parish had its annual 'First Communion Day' when all the seven year olds who had been properly instructed made their first communion together during one of the parish Masses. It is now becoming more and more common to regard first communion as a family occasion. In consultation with the parish priest, each family decides upon the particular Sunday on which they wish their child to make its first communion. If possible, the whole family accompanies the child to the altar where they receive the sacrament together. Younger children and babes in arms are often brought by their parents to the altar at communion time to receive a blessing from the priest.

The Directory then proceeds to discuss how children are to be treated in the liturgical assembly in general. The situation which obtains in this country more or less universally at the present time is that children of all ages are brought to Mass by their parents, so that at nearly every Sunday Mass the celebrant finds himself faced by a representative cross-section of his entire parish, from the very elderly to more or less vociferous babes in arms.

This is no bad thing, since it expresses the nature of the Church as the family of God to which persons of all ages belong. Moreover, the witness given by the adult faithful can have a good effect on the children, and adults themselves can derive much spiritual profit from observing the children's part in the Christian community. It does much to foster a truly Christian spirit in the home.

However, children can be a problem, especially toddlers and crying babies. Some churches have what is called a 'Crying room', a side room screened off from the main church by a soundproof glass partition affording a view of the sanctuary. Here mothers can attend Mass with their very young children and no one in the main church is disturbed. The Directory does not in fact offer this solution. Instead it suggests that infants be taken to a room apart from the main church and left in the care of 'parish helpers' who will look after them until the end of Mass and then bring them into the church for the final blessing with the community.

The children who are present at the Parish Mass must never be allowed to feel neglected through their inability to participate in or understand what is being said and done. Some notice should be taken of them. At the very least the celebrant can say a special word of greeting to them at the beginning and address some part of the sermon specially to them. They can also be given things to do, such as bringing the wine and water to the altar and singing their own hymns on occasions.

Where the necessary facilities are available, it is possible to have a special service of the word for the children in a separate room. They then return to the church for the liturgy of the Eucharist. There are several churches where this is done to good effect, and it is a practice which is well established in churches of other denominations.

The Directory then goes on to consider the conduct of Masses specially for children. Here an extraordinary amount of latitude is allowed under the title of adaptation.

First, with regard to the place of worship. The principle is established that the church is the primary place for a eucharistic celebration with children. It is not, however, necessary to use the nave and main altar. A space within the church could be selected and arranged to suit the number of children participating and the use they will need to make of this space in the celebration of their liturgy. Where this is not possible, another room can be chosen, but one which is suitable and 'worthy of the dignity of the Mass'.

Here the Directory is not in line with current practice in this country where, as we have seen, the classroom Mass has become an established custom, Masses are celebrated in the home, and youth Masses are often celebrated in church halls and youth centres. During the war the displacement of military personnel often made it necessary to celebrate Mass in NAAFI canteens and even public houses, and it was perhaps during that period that our reluctance to use secular buildings for sacred worship was largely overcome. Some relic of the sacred was preserved by the priest taking with him a consecrated 'portable altar-stone' which was put on the table where Mass was said, and on which rested the sacred elements. But, since the revision of the Roman Missal, altar-stones are no longer *de rigueur*.

The Directory discourages the too frequent celebration of Mass with the same group of children. Other regular forms of worship and prayer can be devised to suit their needs.

Great insistence is laid on the need for adequate preparation, both of the children for their worship and of the details of the act of celebration, and specific rules are laid down regarding the adaptation of prayers and chants.

Efforts are being made by competent authorities to produce special eucharistic prayers for children. Until these have been approved, their use is not permitted and one must use one of the four which currently appear in the Roman Missal.

The need for a special eucharistic prayer for children is keenly felt among Catholic educationists in this country, and private compositions have in fact been used in many places. There is a danger that the situation may get out of hand if nothing authoritative is done fairly soon. Some continental countries have already approved children's eucharistic prayers, and they appear printed in their people's missals. A special eucharistic prayer was composed for the Children's Mass at the Eucharistic Congress in Melbourne in 1973. This received official approval from Rome, but only for use on this one occasion. However, Rome has asked local hierarchies to prepare sample 'Children's Canons' and to submit them for possible approval. Meanwhile they have a committee studying the problem.[1]

Another area where the need for adaptation is felt is in the scriptural readings. Old Testament readings and Epistles are notoriously difficult for children to understand, and these may be omitted if suitable alternatives cannot be found in the Roman Lectionary. The Gospel, however, must never be omitted, though sentences of particular difficulty can be left out provided the overall sense is not impaired. The simplified versions of Scripture at present authorized for catechetical use may be employed in the Liturgy for Children, but not 'paraphrases' or re-writes of the Scripture.

Nothing is said about the growing use of non-biblical material in children's worship, although the insistence on the importance of the Word of God and the need to familiarize children with it from an early age would seem to discourage this particular practice. One could conceivably argue that such material could legitimately be used as a modern commentary on the scriptural word, provided it is clear to the children that there is a big difference between the scriptural and the non-scriptural. This distinction might not readily be appreciated by the very young.

Clearly we still have a long road to travel before anything like a permanent solution to these problems is arrived at. We are still in the learning stage, and the experience of other Churches will contribute greatly to a final solution—if there is such a thing as a final solution in a world of changing perspectives. What is certain is that the problem is not confined to the realm of children's worship. It raises the whole question of what precisely is entailed in the newly enunciated principle of a 'pastoral liturgy' and will inevitably have repercussions over the whole area of liturgical celebration.

[1] On 1 November 1974 the Congregation for Divine Worship published the text of three eucharistic prayers for Children's Masses for experimental use until the end of 1977.

5 A METHODIST POINT OF VIEW

A. Raymond George

A child of Methodist parents is normally baptized as an infant; during his childhood he (or she) attends the services of the Church or the sessions of the Sunday school or both, and it is hoped that at some point in his adolescence he will personally confess Jesus Christ as Lord and Saviour. He will then become a Member in Training, he will receive special instruction, and by the vote of the church council of a local church, on the recommendation of its pastoral sub-committee, he will become a full member. He will then be received at a service called Public Reception into Full Membership or Confirmation; this service will end with the Lord's Supper, which he will probably receive for the first time. This process, called Entry into the Church more commonly than Christian Initiation, is, however, at present the subject of a good deal of discussion.

The first problem concerns the relation of the Church to the Sunday school. The Sunday school movement began as an educational and evangelistic agency for unchurched children; it became extremely popular in the last century in Methodism, as in the other Free Churches. Whereas the church services were held on Sunday morning and evening, the Sunday school was held chiefly on Sunday afternoon. Sometimes there were classes for adults as well as for children; the whole institution was almost a rival to the church. Very often there was also a session, less well-attended, before the Sunday morning services; and the children who attended this would be encouraged to stay for the whole or at least the first part of the morning service. The custom then arose that this part of the service would include a children's hymn and a children's address, often at the expense of one of the lessons, and this to some extent distorted the form of the service.

In recent years the fashion has changed. The afternoon session of the Sunday school has been generally abandoned, and there is a widespread custom of holding the Sunday school, often under some such name as Junior Church, at the same time as the morning service. Usually the children, except perhaps the very youngest, attend the service for about ten or fifteen minutes, and during this time, though children's addresses are now hardly ever given, some regard is had to the presence of the children, as by the choice of the second hymn. They then withdraw to their own classes, which finish at the same time as the church service, so that parents and children may return home together. Occasionally, however, the children, except the very youngest, remain throughout, and the service on such Sundays is often called a 'Family Service' and takes a somewhat simpler form. A book *Together in Church*, published by the Methodist Youth Department, contains suggestions for such services, for the services of uniformed organizations such as Scouts and Guides, who usually remain throughout the service, and for the beginning of worship when children are present, as also for the ending, for in some churches they enter towards the end rather than leave after the beginning.

The advantage of this system is that, whereas under the old system many children came only in the afternoon, hardly ever worshipped with the adults, and, except at the Sunday school anniversary, never saw the inside of the church, children now enjoy the corporate worship of the whole local church, young and old alike, though on most Sundays only for ten or fifteen minutes. There are, however, three great disadvantages. One is that the Sunday school teachers, who leave with the children, never attend the rest of the morning service. It is true that they can attend in the evening, but it is not clear how much longer there are likely to be evening services similar in shape to the morning ones. Secondly, this difficulty is accentuated on those Sundays on which morning service ends with the Lord's Supper. The Sunday school session is not likely to end in time for the teachers to re-enter the church and receive the communion. On the other hand, on those Sundays the service is likely to be prolonged a little beyond the end of the Sunday school session, so that young children are left waiting for the emergence of their parents. The third difficulty is that the presence of the children for ten or fifteen minutes raises liturgical problems. Is the church service to be associated in their minds, for instance, almost exclusively with a prayer of confession and an

Old Testament lesson? This difficulty is accentuated by the sug-
gestion that a lesson should be read to harmonize with the theme
which will be followed in their classes. A lesson is published which is
relevant to the British Lessons Council syllabus upon which *Partners
in Learning*, the series of text books for Sunday school lessons, is
based. If this lesson is read in addition to the lessons of the Methodist
Church's official lectionary, it introduces too many lessons; if it
replaces one of them, it even so introduces a second theme into the
service, and often involves putting the New Testament lesson
before the Old; and if it replaces the official lessons entirely, the value
of the Church's official lectionary is lost, the diet of Scripture that
replaces it is somewhat meagre, and the Church's worship is sub-
ordinated to the needs of an educational syllabus. Many ministers
have expressed the hope that the Church's lectionary and the British
Lessons Council syllabus may be in some way assimilated to each
other, and the British Lessons Council syllabus committee, which
is in any case committed to the revision of the syllabus, is fortunately
conferring with the Joint Liturgical Group (on whose lectionary the
Methodist lectionary is based) to this end. Even if an exact correspondence cannot be secured, it is hoped that the two schemes can
at least be brought into general harmony. This would probably be
of greater help to Methodism than to any other Church, for though
Methodists do not follow the lectionary rigidly (and indeed some
do not follow it at all), they probably do so more fully than any of
the other Free Churches which use the BLC syllabus; and the use
of the lectionary is probably increasing.

The solution of all these problems about morning worship is not
easy. One possible solution, often adopted in America, would be to
hold two sessions in the morning, separated by refreshments. They
could be in either order. One would consist of the Sunday morning
worship, which would be attended by all except the very youngest
who would gather elsewhere with only one or two helpers to play
with them. This would include a short 'liturgical' sermon and might
culminate from time to time in the Lord's Supper; if it did not exceed
about fifty minutes it would not overtax the children, who would
thus have the advantage of joining at length in a true act of family
worship which would take some account of their presence but would
not be at all specially 'geared' to them. The other session (which

could come first or second) would consist of classes for children, and groups of various kinds for adults, who might also receive teaching of a more sustained nature than is possible in a short sermon or engage in other activities such as choir practice. This pattern, however, has hardly begun to establish itself in British Methodism.

The other great set of problems about children's worship is linked with the current debate about Entry into the Church or Initiation. Some ministers deplore the fact that children are so rarely present at the Lord's Supper. It is difficult at the age of perhaps seventeen or eighteen to make adolescents feel at home in a rite which they have perhaps never previously seen. But sometimes adolescents and indeed children are present. They may attend a church where the Sunday school children attend the end rather than the beginning of the morning service, or they may attend a church building shared with Anglicans where there is a weekly service of the Parish Communion style, or they may be children who prefer church to Sunday school. The custom slowly arises, in the Anglican manner, of giving such children a blessing at the communion rail. But it is said that children by about the age of twelve feel that this is a childish practice which emphasizes their exclusion from the Lord's Table rather than their place in the Church's fellowship. Why should not Methodists follow the Roman practice of giving communion to children at a very much younger age, or even the Orthodox practice of giving it to them at any age from their baptism onwards? Some have noted the recent trend of thought in Anglicanism which takes the view that Baptism properly admits to Holy Communion, though in fact this has rarely been so without some intervening act of chrism (as with the Orthodox) or Confirmation or some expression of commitment and faith. The further question is raised as to what there is in the Methodist constitution to prevent those who are not yet full members from receiving Holy Communion, and it is suggested that it is only the comparatively recent assimilation of reception into full membership to Anglican Confirmation, in accordance with the gradual process whereby Methodists have become aware of being a Church as well as a collection of societies, which seems to hinder those who are not members from receiving Holy Communion. But this argument ignores the fact that from the time of John Wesley onwards Holy Communion has, generally speaking, been a privilege of members, though Wesley occasionally admitted children after very careful examination. The question that is raised by this debate is whether the reception of Holy Communion is necessarily connected with a mature confession of faith and entry upon the responsibilities which belong to the institutional life of the Church. The Methodist Youth Department presented to the Methodist Conference of 1973 a report which recommended greater flexibility in this matter, but hesitations were expressed by those who feared the long-term effects of such a policy both on Confirmation and on Holy Communion. The report was then referred to the Faith and Order Committee, which in 1975 produced a full report outlining the advantages and disadvantages of such a policy, but not reaching any very definite conclusion. The Church will clearly have to continue to study the whole issue.

Meanwhile, as in other paedo-Baptist Churches, some are troubled either about infant baptism in general or, more commonly, about what is sometimes called 'indiscriminate' baptism, but the Methodist Church in general takes the view that if after careful instruction parents are willing to make solemn promises contained in the service[1] it is not for the minister to refuse to baptize.

These debates about entry into the Church are, however, for the most part long-term issues. The more immediate question is the arrangement of worship in the average Methodist church on Sunday morning.

[1] The service is contained in the booklet *Entry into the Church*, which was authorized by the Methodist Conference of 1974.

6 A UNITED REFORMED POINT OF VIEW

James Todd

Until about thirty years ago local congregations of what is now the United Reformed Church, and which were then Presbyterian or Congregational, provided for the Christian education and training of their children mainly through the 'Sunday school'. Church halls were designed and built for this purpose, often with one large assembly area surrounded by smaller rooms in which classes could meet. The Sunday school was graded into different age groups and staffed by volunteers who were often exceedingly devoted members of the church. It was normally held on Sunday afternoons, when there might also be Bible classes for young people who had grown beyond the Sunday school stage.

A considerable proportion of the children could be expected to come from homes which had otherwise little connection with the church. Their parents were not church members but were glad to send their children to Sunday school, sometimes to get a little peace and quiet themselves on Sunday afternoons but mainly because they wished their children to have some Christian instruction, even if they felt no need or desire to go to church themselves. Children of church members would attend morning service with their parents, the younger ones leaving before the sermon, and then might go again to Sunday school in the afternoon.

Even though the school was staffed by local members of the church there was always the danger that it might exist alongside the church but with little effective relationship to it. It was largely with the aim of overcoming this separation between school and church that the ideas advocated by H. A. Hamilton in his book *The Family Church in Principle and Practice* gained increasing acceptance. The book appeared in 1941 and a number of congregations began to reorganize themselves on 'Family Church' lines. In most churches some provision had already been made for children who came on Sunday mornings, even though most could be expected to attend in the afternoon. Now increasing importance was attached to attendance in the morning, so that the whole local church family could meet together and the work of Christian education be carried on in the setting of the worshipping community.

Today, afternoon Sunday school is the exception rather than the rule. In most of our congregations children come with their parents to the morning service and sit with them during the first fifteen or twenty minutes. Children whose parents do not come will probably sit in a group, often with one of the junior church leaders to whose department they will go later. Ideally the whole church family is present together in the church during this period of worship. The children then leave for their own services, which finish roughly at the same time as the service in the church, so that parents and children can go home together.

The content of the period of worship while all are present will vary from church to church, and to some extent from time to time. It will probably include a couple of hymns, some introductory prayers, possibly a Scripture reading and often a short address by the minister intended primarily for the children. The custom of giving a 'children's address' grew up when there was usually no other provision for children's instruction on Sunday mornings: they were given this slot in the morning service. It is now widely regarded as unnecessary, even undesirable, when the children will shortly be leaving for their own departmental services. There are, however, those who still value the opportunity it gives to the minister of a personal, pastoral contact with the children which he might not otherwise have. On occasions the children may take some special part in the service during this period, which should serve as an introduction to the rest of the worship both in the congregation and in the departments of the Junior Church.

Infant baptisms are normally included in this part of the service. Because baptism means reception into the life of the Church we regard it as important that whenever possible baptisms should take place when the church is assembled for worship; and it seems most appropriate that this should be done when the whole church family, including the children, is present. Our Book of Order for Worship provides, however, that infant baptisms, like baptisms on profession of faith, may come later in the service, in close relation to the prayers and the offertory.

In the departments of the Junior Church—beginners, primary, junior, and senior—the *Partners in Learning* courses are those most commonly used. These are based on the British Lessons Council Syllabus 'Experience and Faith' and are published by the National Christian Education Council and the Methodist Church Division of Education and Youth. They aim to ensure that all sections of the church are dealing with the same general theme on any particular Sunday. The problem of the relation of these courses to the sequence of the Christian Year and to the lessons provided in the Lectionary, where that is followed, is one that we have to face in our churches but is outside the scope of this paper.

The Family Church pattern for morning worship means that, on most Sundays, the children are not present during the greater part of the service in the church. With a few exceptions they are also present during the celebration of the Lord's Supper, which is usually celebrated monthly. Very few of our churches regularly welcome children of all ages to receive communion; some arrange for them to be present as non-communicants, either regularly or on special occasions; the majority reserve full participation in the sacrament for those who have been through a course of preparation for membership and have been confirmed, or 'received into communicant membership'.

The traditional link between admission to the Lord's Supper and participation in the Church Meeting (especially in former Congregational churches) has meant that young people are not usually confirmed at as early an age with us as in some other churches, though the tendency today is to admit them at a younger age than formerly, probably at thirteen or fourteen. A good deal of discussion is at present going on in our Church about the whole question of the presence of children at Communion. It is likely that a report about this will be presented to our General Assembly in the near future. Two considerations in particular call for comment:

1. While the advantage of bringing the whole church family together for an initial period of family worship will be obvious, the long-term result of encouraging the children to go out to their own departments has been to organize them out of public worship. When they reach the age of finishing with Junior Church they have had little if any experience of attending a full service of worship with the

congregation, and no discipline in doing so. Many stop coming alto-
gether. We try to overcome this by giving them a job to do as helpers
or teachers in Junior Church, or by arranging a youth group for
them; but we are almost back again at the trouble from which the
concept of Family Church was meant to deliver us: the divorce
between Sunday school and church.

2. A second disadvantage of our present arrangement is that
children share in the congregation's worship only during the introductory part of the service. They are not there at the climax of
worship. In some of our churches an attempt is made to overcome
this by bringing them back into the church for the last ten or fifteen
minutes. In this case, they are in their departments during the
Scripture readings and the sermon, and return for the prayers, the
offering, the final hymn, and the blessing. This, of course, consider-
ably reduces the time available in the departments, unless the
minister preaches far longer than most congregations would endure
today. It also interrupts the service unless very few children are
involved, which is all too often unhappily the case.

There is probably no single, ideal solution to these and other
problems. Conditions vary from church to church, in numbers of
adults and children involved and in type and convenience of buildings. What is most important is that children should be made to
feel that they are part of the living, worshipping community of God's
people. To quote H. A. Hamilton:

> Providing that children have opportunities for worship which is
> a fulfilment of their separate interests, it is of quite critical import-
> ance that they should share in worship with the whole family of
> God and come into the sense of a family together before Him. It is
> impossible to overestimate how much children have lost because
> their religious education has been carried on, in the main, solely
> in the departmental group. Nothing must ever allow us to diminish
> the value of working and thinking with them in age groups and
> interest groups, but neither must anything prevent us from
> finding speedily the best way of including them in the family
> life of the Church when that family is in the presence of God.[1]

[1] *The Family Church in Principle and Practice*, p. 32.

7 A BAPTIST POINT OF VIEW

Stephen Winward

Most Baptist churches accept the obligation of teaching children. In the recent past, the teaching has been given in Sunday schools meeting on Sunday afternoons, with only a small minority of children attending morning services. The weakness of this arrangement was that children could receive instruction for years without meeting the congregation, except on rare occasions. In the last few decades there has been a widespread attempt to overcome this separation by abolishing the afternoon Sunday school and adopting morning Family Church. The usual pattern today is for children to worship with the congregation on Sunday mornings for some fifteen to twenty minutes and then to withdraw into departments and classes for instruction. In a minority of churches the children join the congregation for the climax of the service; in a few churches they are present both at the beginning and at the end. While the children are in church there will be one or two hymns, the Scripture lesson(s), and prayer(s). The custom of giving a children's address, once almost universal, is now on the wane. In many churches there is little or no relationship between the church service and the subsequent departmental instruction. Other churches attempt a unity of presentation for the children either by relating the first part of the service to their subsequent lesson, or by imposing that lesson on the whole congregation throughout the service. The church then tends to become one big Sunday school with lections and sermons set by the children's lesson for the day. Some follow the Calendar and Lectionary, not unduly concerned that the instruction given to the children may be unrelated provided that it bears a general overall correspondence to the pattern of the Christian Year. On this issue there are still unresolved tensions and problems.

The Lord's Supper is for believers only; the Lord's Supper is for baptized believers only. In the past, the practice of Baptist churches has been determined by one or other of these two convictions. Since children were not believers and had not been baptized, they were not present at the Communion. They are not usually present today. If they meet with the congregation on an occasion when the Supper is to be administered, they leave at some point before Communion. The general practice is to have Communion in the evening on the first Sunday of the month, and in the morning on the third Sunday. These celebrations take place *after* another full-length service. The preaching service ends with the Benediction, and those who are not communicating leave before the Communion. If, on occasions, children stay in church throughout the preaching service, they will still leave, together with some adults, before the Communion. A child can grow up in a Baptist church without ever having been present at the Supper.

It is a minority of churches which have departed from the traditional pattern of Sunday worship which are confronted with the problem of children at the Communion. In some churches the Lord's Supper is celebrated as the main weekly morning service on the Lord's Day. In other churches the monthly morning celebration has been integrated with the service of the Word to make one service. There is no 'break' during which the non-communicants leave. There is a tendency, at the festivals, for children to stay in church throughout the morning service including the Communion. In a few places children return from the departments to be present with the congregation for the Communion. Again, the children of some families, and especially if they are visitors, do not leave the congregation for departmental instruction. For these various reasons children are now sometimes, and in some churches often, at Communion. Some pastors appear to regard this as desirable largely for didactic reasons. It is necessary for the upbringing of our children that they should become familiar with the whole range of Christian worship. For others, education is not of primary importance. The children should be with the People of God, assembled to celebrate the sacrifice and victory of Christ. That is when they will become aware of his mysterious presence and meet him in the midst of his people.

Our problem with children at Communion stems from the fact that we now separate two things which in our tradition were joined together. For us, to be present at a Communion service is one thing, and to communicate is another. For our fathers, 'admission to Communion' meant both, and the admission was related by some to belief, and by others to belief and baptism. That baptism should be administered to believers only is a basic conviction of all Baptists. But what is essential for admission to Communion—the belief, or the belief and the baptism administered on confession of faith? From the middle of the seventeenth century two convictions have existed side by side, and there have been closed-Communion and open-Communion churches. Some have believed and taught that only people baptized as believers should be admitted to Communion. Others have believed and taught that believers' baptism is not *essential* for admission to Communion. Faith is the essential, and so they welcome and invite all who believe in the Lord Jesus Christ to the Lord's Table. This second conviction has largely prevailed over the first. Most Baptists today believe in and practise open-Communion, inviting all believers to communicate. On the other hand, there has been some movement in the other direction. Recent Baptist scholarship has emphasized the relationship between Baptism and the Church. This has led some to question a purely individualistic approach to admission to Communion. They believe that the Sacrament of the Body should be received only by those who have been baptized into the one Body. First Baptism, then Communion.

The presence of children at Communion in an open-Communion Baptist church presents a real problem. They have been admitted to the Communion service—are they to communicate? The answer is likely to be: if they are believers, yes; if they are not yet believers, no. And the child himself must make the decision. That's the problem! It is not overcome by 'fencing the Table', i.e. making clear at every service in the words of invitation the conditions on which people may receive the elements. For the invitation given in open-Communion churches to 'all those who believe in our Lord and Saviour Jesus Christ' is not without difficulties when children are present. Many a child could sincerely receive communion on these conditions. When does a child become a believer? Are we insisting on a conversion experience? Do we require repentance and faith? And what has the belief on which we insist to do with age, with understanding, with discretion, with maturity? These questions have to be faced in connection with the administration of believers' baptism. They become even more pressing for those churches which invite to Communion without requiring baptism.

It is asking a lot of a child to place the onus of making the decision, whether or not to communicate, on him. The problem is accentuated by our method of serving the elements which we have inherited from the time when 'admission to Communion' meant that all those present at the service were there to communicate. In most Baptist churches, the elements of bread and wine are distributed by the deacons to the people as they sit in their places. It is easier to stay in your place instead of going up to the Table, than it is to stay in your place and *not* receive the gifts which are brought to you. In such circumstances a child needs to know beyond doubt whether or not he is eligible to communicate. This is not a problem in those churches which teach and require children and young people to be baptized before they communicate. The merit of this position is its clarity. A young person knows whether or not he has been baptized as a believer, and thus knows whether or not he is eligible to communicate. In such a church all children and young people grow up with the clear understanding—first Baptism, then the Lord's Supper.

8 A CHURCHES OF CHRIST POINT OF VIEW

W. G. Baker

1. In Churches of Christ the regular congregational weekly worship is a service of Holy Communion which, in its basic structure, is similar to the pattern outlined in the Joint Liturgical Group booklet *Initiation and Eucharist*.

2. Members of the Church are those who are baptized following their own voluntary decision and the teaching which has led up to that point; or those who have become members of a Church of Christ congregation as 'ecumenical members'. ('Ecumenical membership may be generally defined as membership of a Church of Christ allowed to those who come without having been baptised as believers by immersion but who are already members of some branch of the Christian church.' Some people have been baptized in infancy but have not become communicant members of their own churches, for example, by Confirmation; we do not feel that we should decide about the status of, for instance, those baptized in an Anglican church but who have not been confirmed. For this reason our view of ecumenical membership relates only to those who are full communicant members of their own church.)

3. It will be seen then that in Churches of Christ young children are not participating fully in the congregation's regular weekly worship.

4. For children of church members there has normally been a 'Service of Thanksgiving for Childbirth and Dedication of Parents' —and this applies also where only one parent is a church member. While this acknowledges a special relationship of the child to the Church, it is not of course Baptism, which is what constitutes membership of the Church. (Infants of families which are related to the educational and social activities of the local church are usually brought to a Cradle Roll Service, in which they are linked with the

educational and social fellowship of the Church, and this service can be the beginning of Christian commitment by the parents.)

5.   Worship, for the children, is therefore in 'attendance' at congregational worship and in the experience of the evangelistic, educational, pastoral, and social activities which the Church provides both on Sunday and through the week. In this there is normally a carefully planned programme of teaching and experience which includes worship—worship specially prepared for appropriate ages and occasions. This worship is normally in Sunday schools, youth groups, and other local church auxiliaries.

Various syllabuses are used, but for many years Churches of Christ have generally used those of the British Lessons Council and now a considerable proportion of the Churches use the *Partners in Learning* handbooks. These Guides are recommended by the education department of Churches of Christ as also are the Guides *Alive in God's World* and the . . . *in the Church* series published by the St Andrew's Press. (Here and there some Guides are used which give us some concern!)

6.   Regarding the regular weekly worship, that is, the celebration of Holy Communion, it has not been our custom to encourage the deforming of the service by interpolating 'little bits for children, after which they can depart'. That this practice, common in many churches, but not always fully thought through, would take away many of the teachers from Holy Communion is not the least of its weaknesses!

7.   Nevertheless, the children's attendance, observance, and experience at Holy Communion are increasingly considered to be highly important in the development of the child's spiritual life and of his sense of the fellowship of the church family.

8.   This, therefore, has led to 'Family Worship', in which children more truly share in the eucharistic morning service, without of course communicating. Because there is a serious attempt to think through the concept of Family Worship, this practice is essentially different from the somewhat sentimental and casual happening referred to in paragraph 6. Of fifty of our Churches which declared that they shared in 'Family Worship' of this kind, twenty-four have

this occasionally; fifteen monthly; and five as a normal part of weekly worship. As far as we know, there are no congregations in whose worship children who have not been baptized take communion.

9. In Churches of Christ, at Holy Communion, the bread and the wine are brought to the congregation by servers and passed along the pews as individuals partake of them. If children and known non-communicants are sitting in one group, with no communicant among them, then usually the servers will not offer the elements to them. Where there are children sitting among communicants, the children will simply hand on the plate and the cup without partaking of the bread and the wine.

Many congregations are aware of the value of the whole natural family's gathering together 'at the altar rail', as it were, as in the Church of England Family Communion. Some of the congregations are trying to devise some appropriate symbolic action which can involve both the natural family and the whole congregation as a church family. So far, however, no completely satisfactory action has been suggested.

10. In Churches of Christ we also seek to express this worship of the whole church family together in a way in which worship and education, on themes related to the Lectionary, comprehend the entire age range. The current phrase to describe this seems to be 'Church Community Education'; but one can assume that the Churches do not think of the essentially eucharistic liturgy as being primarily educational!

11. If, however—as we would wish—the total educational experience of the child in the Church is grounded in the Church's eucharistic worship, then we should wish to sustain the integration of worship and education. Some people think that we must choose between (i) using the Joint Liturgical Group Lectionary and making up an educational syllabus which fits it, or (ii) not using the Lectionary, and somehow relating the eucharistic worship to the use (in Sunday school and elsewhere) of some generally accredited syllabus of Christian education.

12. As Churches of Christ generally use the Joint Liturgical Group

Lectionary, it means that more work must be done in using in the service of the Word devotional and educational material based on the Lectionary. This also requires an appropriately related syllabus of Christian education for use in the Sunday school and other agencies of the Church. It must be said that not the easiest of tasks before the Churches is that of training Sunday school teachers and other leaders of the children to relate their service and worship at the Eucharist to a teaching programme which is not pedagogic only, but which truly brings together 'Worship and the Child'.

Neville Clark

The documents of liturgical renewal have had little enough to say about children. It is arguable that by that omission seeds of potential disaster have been only too effectively sown. To juxtapose 'The child' and 'Worship' is to produce a combination of emphases that falls unexpectedly on too many ears. For this is not a natural connection for the modern Church to make.

It is important to seek the reason for this situation. Doubtless there are many. Yet the most significant of them is surely that, within the general Christian community, inherited memories of dealing with children are bound up primarily with the institution traditionally known as the Sunday school. If this diagnosis is in any way sound, the implications of it must bear scrutiny.

The Sunday schools of the nineteenth century were quite clear and realistic about their task. They engaged themselves in teaching children to read and write, and then—when an age of wider literacy dawned—in passing on the elements of the Christian Faith to children who lacked the privilege of a Christian home. They knew themselves to be inadequate substitutes for the Christian family. Their emphasis, accordingly, was a modest one. It was upon instruction. It is this concern that has heavily governed the thinking of the Church in connection with children ever since. The difference now is that we do not call it instruction. We call it education.

The distinction at this point should be neither unfairly exaggerated nor improperly minimized. The shift from instruction to education is the indicator that reflects the new thinking about children, their growth, and their learning process, that has gone on over recent decades. Instruction tended to work with the model of the child as a receptacle into which slices of knowledge were to be inserted. Education speaks of a process of leading and discovery whereby the child, his interest aroused, is put in the way of learning, and is encouraged to deeper understanding through widening

experience. The difference is real. Equally obvious, however, is
the fact that whether the emphasis be on instruction or on education
it is basically on learning. The overriding concern is not the child
and worship. It is the child and learning.

That this is so becomes more than usually apparent when attention
is paid to contemporary disputes about the use of the Bible with
children. On the one side it is argued that the Bible is not a children's
book, that the unreflecting teaching of biblical material implants in
the child's mind all kinds of misunderstandings and misconceptions
about the Christian Faith which block the road to mature faith and
positively encourage rejection of Christianity when adolescence is
reached. So the concern is all for ordinary, everyday experience.

Scripture is sparingly and cautiously used. It is introduced to
illustrate human situations and issues of common life. On the other
hand, the opponents of this view will argue that the Bible is being
sold short, and that children are being left in ignorance of its riches.
The cry is for a return to straight scriptural teaching that starts with
the Bible, ends with the Bible, and keeps the Bible central.

It sounds like a specific and particularly important instance of the
familiar battle between education and instruction. In a way it is.
Yet is has more fearful dimensions. For the supremely significant
thing revealed by it is that, in the end, both parties operate with the
same ground rules. Learning is the preoccupation, not worship.
And not infrequently both parties, logically enough, tend to have
imperialistic designs upon the 'adult' service of worship, and are
eager to tilt the liturgy dramatically in the direction of their own
particular learning model. The 'educationists' complain bitterly of
the medieval nature of worship where people sit and listen to a Word
addressed to them, and object that the whole process is educationally nonsensical. The 'instructionists' increasingly extol the virtues
of the all-age Sunday school, and are sometimes prepared to urge the
curtailment of worship, if necessary, in order to subject the adults to
the instruction given, at simplified level, to the children. From both
directions a take-over bid is made. Whatever the shape of the
palace, learning is king.

All this is not the assumption of the few—those perhaps who deal
with children in the church context. Rather is this the assumption of
the many. The uncovering of what is at stake may perhaps be more

clearly achieved by the posing of some key questions. Does what is done with the children on Sunday mornings really prepare them over the years for real participation in the worshipping assembly of the People of God? Is the transition in the early 'teens from Sunday school or Junior Church to Service of Worship a smooth one because taken by prepared people who are simply advancing a further step along the same track? Or does it seem to them like a sudden unconnected jerk from one kind of activity to another?

That such questions are real and searching is indicated by two significant and common attitudes. A generation that has passed through the traditional Sunday school tends to find it particularly difficult to understand the true nature of worship. Almost inevitably the assessment of it is likely to be made in instructional terms. Too easily worship may be viewed as essentially a form of adult instruction. Where this happens the emphasis is laid upon the sermon, for which hymns, prayers, and the like constitute a kind of preparation. And the function of the sermon is seen to be instructional. 'What have I learned today?' becomes the question. 'Was it clear and understandable?' becomes the criterion. The underlying assumption is that what the children get on *their* level the adult should be getting on *his*.

The other common attitude is equally interesting. It is likely to be found among the generation which has passed through some variations of the more modern 'Family Church' system, most widely practised in the Free Churches. Equally there is likely to be a problem of understanding the real nature of worship. Equally liturgy may be viewed as basically a form of adult education. The difference is that now the 'adult' service is likely to be criticized on the ground that it is educationally out of date. Children are being dealt with on sound educational principles. Informality is encouraged. Discussion takes place. Activity is all. And then—the teenager is suddenly thrown back into the dark ages and made to sit still on a chair, keep quiet for much of the time, and listen.

Here then are two different attitudes, widely represented within the Christian community. The space between them is vast. Yet it is not the distinction that finally impresses. For underlying both is the one familiar and crucial assumption already identified. Whether for the child or for the adult, education, instruction, learning, is the name of the game.

But is it? Or is the name of the game really worship? It may assist towards the reaching of firm conclusions to inquire what is our goal for the child. Surely the concern is that the children shall, in years of understanding, respond to the call and claim of God and commit their lives to him. Clearly—and fortunately—such a commitment cannot be stage-managed or coerced. It can, however, be prepared for so that in due time a conscious and understanding confrontation with God becomes possible. How is such preparation to be made?

Certainly the presence, challenge, and claim of God can be known and experienced in all sorts of strange places. Commitment to God can be made in the most unlikely circumstances. All this is finally—and fortunately—beyond human control. Yet none of this alters the fact that what might fairly be called the 'familiar' point of confrontation with God is the corporate worship of the Church. There is nothing surprising or accidental about that. For this is precisely the thing with which the Liturgy is concerned.

Such a confrontation with God in corporate worship is, of course, an indirect one. What else could it be? God is not a visiting preacher who could be ushered in, pointed out, introduced, and invited to 'say a few words'. No one has 'seen' God. Any confrontation has to take place *through* something or someone else. In the Liturgy, that 'something else' is focally and centrally the biblical tradition. The Word is proclaimed in Scripture and in sermon in order that a highway be opened that may become 'the way of the Lord'.

Nor is this the whole. In praise and prayer it is the presence of God which is being sought and celebrated. In the Eucharist it is the presence of God in Christ which is being expected, anticipated, and received. From first to last corporate worship is concerned with an encounter with God which offers life and claims commitment.

It is *all this* for which the child is being prepared. At this point the Christian community has discharged its task faithfully when through the years it has made a child 'ready' for a conscious confrontation with God in corporate worship. Yet if this is the goal and the concern, there seems something more than a little odd about the desperate eagerness in too many places to remove the children from that worship. To keep them strangers to the Liturgy for as many years as possible would appear to be a curious kind of 'preparation'.

In not a few quarters even to raise this issue is to unleash a barrage

of outraged argument. The 'adult' service is no place for the children
—at least, not for more than fifteen minutes. They will be bored.
They will be fidgety. They will be unhappy. They will revolt. They
will come to loathe the whole enterprise. Are we still in the nineteenth century? Have we learned nothing from the educationists?
The attack seems overwhelming. Where infants are concerned,
part of it may well have proper force. Yet it may be worth while to
probe deeper and attempt to disentangle the issues. For it seems
likely that a wide range of presuppositions are being paraded.

Certainly it is true that were the aim instruction we should be
criminally foolish to encourage children to be present at the
Liturgy. We have, however, already argued that worship is not a
form of adult education. 'What have I learned today?' is quite the
wrong question for any worshipper to ask as he stumbles out after
the Blessing. The central concern of corporate worship is the presence, coming, challenge, and claim of God. It is not immediately
apparent that this is necessarily irrelevant to everybody under the
age of fourteen.

Other hesitations seem to be bound up with a curious preoccupation with intelligibility. Taken to its extreme this would
result in the conclusion that children should not be confronted with
things they do not understand. Yet few positions can be more out-
dated than that. Any educationist could drive a coach and horses
through it with one hand tied behind his back. In reality all sensible
parents know that the child develops precisely because in the
family he is not insulated from everything beyond his own level
of experience and understanding. It would be odd if the Church
at the heart of its life were to stand inflexibly for a diametrically
opposite position.

There is, of course, no virtue in deliberate and sustained un-
intelligibility. If corporate worship were (or is) a matter of sitting
still for an hour and listening to an intellectual address, then woe
betide the child (and the adult as well). But if the Liturgy is a mixture
of activities all of which are designed to act as a highway along which
God meets his children, then we dare not too quickly or lightly
exclude the child.

It might seem attractive at this point to follow relentlessly the
apparent logic of the argument and claim that all children of all ages

should be present for the total act of corporate worship Sunday by Sunday. To make such a leap would, however, be to move too slickly and easily. In any event the primary aim must be to uncover relevant governing principles. For reasons that will emerge diversity of practical application is likely to prove necessary and inevitable.

What is this corporate worship to which we seek to introduce our children? It is that central Liturgy of the Church which is built round the twin poles of Word and Supper. Should the children be present at the celebration of the Supper? Certainly experience at many a Parish Communion would prompt an affirmative answer. To bring the child from earliest years into intimate touch with the beating heart of Christian worship may be to offer him a gift of incalculable worth.

Nevertheless, no unqualified plea in this direction can or should be made. A divided Church manifests divergent eucharistic theologies which themselves contribute to differences of eucharistic practice. All this is not simply to be ignored when the matter of the presence of children at the Supper and their participation in it is an issue. Some eucharistic understandings may allow the child to 'communicate' equally with the adult. Others may confine the sharing of the Supper to the 'committed' membership and radically call into question any non-communicating attendance. At these extremes the implications for the child are at least clear-cut.

The most difficult decisions are likely to arise in the area in-between, in those church situations where theology on the one hand debars the full participation of the child, yet on the other hand combines with a strong sense of the 'family' character of the Church to encourage his presence. Two possibilities then emerge. Either the bread and wine are simply withheld from the child or he is offered what is felt to be some fitting 'substitute'. Both practices demand scrutiny.

The Eucharist reaches its fullness and fulfilment in 'Communion'. There is accordingly always a sense in which non-communicating attendance fundamentally denies the focal intent of the celebration. To take this fact seriously is not to rule out all such attendances on all occasions. It is to put a serious question mark against the deliberate institution and regular encouragement of such attendance on the part of one group within the Christian community. Certainly it may be argued that what is being offered is a form of 'spiritual' communion. Yet it has then to be asked why a group that is adjudged capable of and apt for this somewhat hazy reality must be debarred from the more regular form of *communio in sacris*.

A more powerful case is likely to be made along the lines of the enormous significance of setting the child in the context of the full eucharistic celebration. Will not the riches of corporate worship make their impact upon him here with unexampled force? Will he not be exposed in this way to influences the range and force of which cannot finally be measured? Will he not by this means be brought to look after and long for the eventual fullness of what he is enabled dimly and partially to experience?

The argument is a powerful one. It catches completely the insight that worship does not operate wholly at the conscious level. It gives proper recognition to the truth that familiarity with the Eucharist over the years can potently assist in preparation for the eventual and meaningful participation in it. Yet still questions must be pressed. On the one hand, theological objections to the proposed practice, in so far as it is regular rather than occasional, must be seriously weighed. On the other hand, the extent to which spurious sentimentality may be replacing sober judgement must be realistically envisaged. The understanding of the Church in terms of the image of the modern family has been far too slickly provided with a New Testament imprimatur, and the liturgical corollaries drawn from that image demand relentless questioning. It may well be that the case for non-communicating attendance of children at the Eucharist can be made. It is not, however, clear that it has yet been made.

The other possibility remains. It is that the child from whom the bread and wine are withheld should be present at the Eucharist and, at the point of 'communion', be offered some appropriate substitute. Here once more the reservations crowd in. What is a Christian community in fact saying to itself and to its children in such a situation? Powerful and convincing reasons can be given for the attempt to draw the children into the worshipping assembly and to set them at the heart of the liturgical action. Yet the problem and the peril of offering them at the climactic moment 'a pat and a blessing' and thereby something *other than* the corporate worship of the People of

God should surely be plain. And if such a distinction is made solely in the case of *children*, the danger is compounded. As always, it is fatally easy to embrace apparently attractive practices in harmony with modern sentiment before the theological, liturgical, and psychological realities have been searchingly weighed.

We have affirmed that the Liturgy is built round the twin poles of Word and Supper. We have glimpsed the problems and possibilities bound up with the presence of children at the Supper. How does it stand with them in relationship to the Word?

To answer that question convincingly will require a closer and keener examination of what the Church should be seeking to do for and with its children. If the concern is the preparation of the child for response and commitment to the call and claim of God, then the goal is Christian 'formation', and the road is Christian 'nurture'. There is a 'Tradition' into which the child is to enter, so that in and through it the encounter with God in Jesus Christ may take place. When the life of the Church is healthy and strong, it is the place where the Tradition of the People of God is effectively handed on in such manner as to illumine, disturb, and transfigure developing experience and elicit appropriate responses and commitments.

It should be emphasized that this handing on of the Tradition is not the transfer of a packaged body of knowledge. The Tradition is a living thing, though not formless or lacking in content. No passive, uncritical reception is involved but rather an engagement which leaves neither partner untouched. The Tradition has form but is constantly being re-formed. To receive it is to enter into it, to experience Christian 'formation' by being progressively initiated into the ethos and mores of the People of God. It is not to achieve mastery of a corpus of belief so much as to obtain the freedom of a city. It is to find a standing ground and gain a perspective and explore a new world which promises to become home.

Clearly every aspect of the corporate life of the Church should assist the process of Christian formation. Equally clearly the liturgical assembly is a supreme vehicle of that formation. In the Liturgy the Tradition is being crucially and centrally handled and unleashed; for Scripture permeates the Liturgy, and Scripture is the normative focus of the Tradition. As the Word is proclaimed in Scripture and sermon, the Tradition moves massively into the centre of the arena.

For the Bible is not essentially a deposit of truth to be conveyed, but the witness to a constant reinterpretation of the Tradition as in each fresh critical situation God grapples with his People.

So it is that when the Word is truly proclaimed in the Liturgy the Tradition is set in motion and becomes a living thing. A search-light plays upon human horizons. Present experience is grasped by the future of God. A new world supervenes upon an old. Such at least is the intention, the hope, and the prayer. Certainly it is the whole man including mind and imagination that is confronted. Yet the essential thrust is upon the will. Only incidentally and peripherally can the response be: Now I understand! Now I know! Centrally and substantially it is to be: This is where I belong—and, this being how things are, now I must choose.

It is against such a background of understanding that the place of the child is to be assessed. Three key terms demand constant attention and proper interrelatedness—exposure, readiness, and preparation. As the Church deals with its children, it must never lose sight of its primary responsibility to 'prepare' them for response and commitment to the call and claim of God. Such preparation involves continuing 'exposure' to the living Tradition from earliest years. Yet while the Tradition can and should make a profound impact below the conscious level, it is not simply an indefinable atmosphere. It also has content. So it is that the 'readiness' of the child for engagement with it becomes significant at every stage of the journey. Too easily that readiness can be lacking, or worse still can suffer distortion.

This is why the 'movement' of Christian formation must be carefully and sensitively observed. It is the movement *from* exposure to the Tradition *to* conscious confrontation with the Tradition. How is that movement to be made?

Where the parents are Christians, it is in the Christian family that exposure to the Tradition will and should begin. Equally, it is there that the readiness of the child for a conscious confrontation with the Tradition will take initial shape or suffer initial distortion. The stakes are high. The demands, however, are not impossible. What is required of the Christian family is not a highly articulated understanding of the Faith or a sophisticated domestic practice of its disciplines, however praiseworthy and desirable these things may be. Rather is the family required to be the place where the Tradition and the twentieth century meet in fruitful interplay to create a quality of being and a style of living which may mediate and bring near to the child that world which the Tradition bears.

Within the Church context, such exposure to the Tradition must continue. This at least means that from earliest years the child may find a place within the liturgical assembly and be present at part of its activity. For worship is not only the proclamation of the Word. Rather is it a totality of action every part of which is controlled and coloured by the Tradition since it is the Tradition that provides the script for the liturgical drama. From first to last in corporate worship a drama is being enacted, a Presence is being realized, a story is being told. To be part of the worshipping community at prayer and praise is to deepen that exposure to the pressures of the presence of God already experienced within the family circle. It is to continue an exposure which may prepare the way for a conscious confrontation in later years at the point of the proclamation of the Word.

But there are other requirements. Facility with the grammar and syntax of the Tradition must be gained. Within the Christian community the Tradition is borne crucially and most explicitly by the proclamation of the Word. It means the introduction of a language world in which the child must one day move with comparative freedom. Only if this is accomplished can the confrontation be expected to take place with power. How is this basic literacy to be achieved? In the last resort it may be gained by participation in the Liturgy itself. The child learns to speak and handle the language as he lives within a family that communicates in his native tongue. In this way Christian literacy *may* be achieved. It cannot, however, be concluded that it *will* be achieved. One hour a week within the worshipping community, many of whose members themselves still stumble over the grammar and syntax, offers but limited opportunity. Some more deliberate provision may be judged necessary.

Even beyond this the contours of the Tradition must impose themselves and become familiar. To gain a purchase on a new language world is not enough. The landmarks of that world need to be known and identified. Again, this *may* in the last resort be accomplished through participation in the Liturgy itself. But again, it cannot be assumed that it will thus be accomplished. It is the old problem of the wood and the trees; and in that Scripture is the normative witness to the Tradition, it is a problem that is focused in the encounter with the Bible. Scripture lessons may be read and expounded. Yet too often they are heard by those who lack familiarity with the total context which gives them life. They descend on waiting ears like strange visitants lacking both ancestry and progeny. Where the proper overview of the Tradition is lacking, its impact is likely to be disastrously blunted. It is when the shape of the Tradition is known that a satisfactory conscious confrontation with it becomes more than an outside possibility. To provide the child with a picture of the biblical landscape is to assist his initiation into the world the Tradition bears.

To take such considerations seriously is to be pressed towards responsible and delicate decisions as to the age at which a child should be encouraged to be present at the Liturgy for Scripture readings and sermon. The issue has only been by-passed, not met, where for other reasons the true proclamation of the Word has been replaced by a 'brief address' which children may reasonably be expected to 'sit through'. More profound realities are at stake than this. Within the Liturgy the child may find his exposure to the Tradition clarified and heightened. He may also begin to assimilate the Tradition's grammar and syntax and find its total shape bodied forth before him, so that in due time a conscious confrontation with the Tradition may take place in meaningful fashion.

Yet preparedness for a grappling with the Tradition is bound up with a literacy and an overview which are only gradually to be obtained and which many adults in the worshipping community itself may only falteringly and partially possess. A tension is revealed of which the child is the most obvious focus. He needs constant experience of the liturgical assembly that he may be continually exposed to the Tradition. Yet he may need withdrawal from the proclamation of the Word in order that he may be deliberately prepared and made ready for that critical confrontation with the Tradition that is concentrated there.

To lose sight of that tension and the precise nature of it is the short road to disaster in the making of any alternative provision for the children at the time of the liturgical assembly on the Lord's Day. If the child is to be withdrawn from the Liturgy at any point, then what is done for him and with him must at all costs be conformed to the nature and thrust of the liturgical activity itself. The learning model must never be allowed to infiltrate and control. Scripture must be seen and used not as a quarry of ideas or beliefs or directives but as the normative witness to the living Tradition into which the child is being initiated. It must be used in such a manner that it speaks of that living Tradition and points to the Lord of that Tradition and the community which is its bearer.

To approach the child in his temporary separation from the Liturgy from such a perspective is to glimpse the lineaments of that response which is required of him. Hitherto the thrust of the argument might have encouraged the conclusion that the child was to be viewed simply as an adult in the making, doomed to suffer his exposure, learn his grammar and syntax, and obtain his overview solely in order that one day he might emerge from the process into a totally new situation of challenge and response. Nothing could be further from the truth. Each step of the way has its own significance. At every stage of the pilgrimage a claim is to be made and a response invited. Here once more the pattern of the Liturgy casts its shadow before it. The commitments to be made may be infinitely varied, provided only that they do not violate the integrity of the growing child. Yet to use Scripture liturgically and faithfully is to be given guidelines which indicate the shape of the goal towards which the Tradition presses. As the Bible engages the growing experience of the child, the crucial response that it seeks is not: 'This I have learned today', but something much more like: 'This is my life. These are my People'.

In the end what emerges is not a uniform programme or solution, but rather an attitude, a signpost, an understanding, a goal. The aim of the Church in the coming days must be to maximize the child's involvement in the Liturgy not minimize it. His withdrawal at points in the Liturgy may be adjudged necessary. Yet if and where such a decision is made, alternative provision must sensibly conform to the liturgical reality and not be shaped by other models or criteria.

Nor, when the child is present within the liturgical assembly, may the Church quickly and lightly offer him something different, go juvenile for ten minutes, or substitute for worship a few spoonfuls of elementary instruction. True worship speaks of mystery, with heights and depths that none of us can fathom. We are being exposed to realities which hit us and meet us at levels below the conscious mind. To expose the child to all that may be a dangerous business, but dangerous probably for reasons quite other than we usually imagine.

If we are honest we may have to confess that some of our hesitations are sheerly practical, though none the less real for that. Our peace may be disturbed. We shall be distracted by the constant effort of ensuring that the child observes 'proper behaviour'. Being a child he is unpredictable. He may wriggle. He may move. He may break the solemnity. And should not worship be solemn?

Yet there may be a more profound obstacle. Deep down in our hearts we surely know two things. One is that if God is to break through in worship to the child it is likely to be through *us*. The other is that our children always know when we are involved in something that really is of life and death significance to us. They may not understand it. It may remain largely a mystery to them. But it is a mystery shot through with its own queer meaning, because it matters to us and matters desperately.

This is the frightening dilemma. Will they be bored because basically we are too? If so, then to keep them in corporate worship might be disastrous, though for reasons quite other than the ones traditionally advanced. What if the only worship we have to offer to our children is so intellectualized that it cannot ring bells with them! What if we cannot guarantee to them a worshipping congregation so fully and desperately involved in playing out the Liturgy that it would communicate to them a sense of the wonder, the joy, and the mystery of God!

The problems remain. Yet two things may be tolerably clear. Whatever we do with the child when and if he withdraws from the Liturgy, we must seek to make room for God to engage his growing experience and elicit his limited response, and we must strive to make him ready for that conscious confrontation with God which corporate worship may one day bring. And when he is present in the sanctuary, we must offer him authentic worship, not some distortion or juvenile corruption of it. So that when at least he comes to take his place as a full participant in the total liturgical action, he may come not as a stranger but as a traveller coming home.